Looking at
Animals
in
LAKES
and
RIVERS

Moira Butterfield

Belitha Press

Introduction

Rivers, lakes, streams and ponds are freshwater places. This means the water is not salty as it would be in a sea or an ocean. There are freshwater places all over the world.

Lots of animals of all shapes and sizes live in or around lakes and rivers. There are tiny insects, strange-looking fish, colourful birds and even big, fierce animals such as crocodiles.

All these animals have their own ways of living in freshwater places.

Contents

Trout

Trout swim along in rivers and lakes
looking for small fish and tadpoles
to gobble up. Female trout lay
tiny eggs on the riverbed.

The baby fish that hatch from the eggs
are called fry. Fishermen like to catch
trout because they are good to eat.

Kingfisher

A kingfisher is a brightly-coloured little bird that lives by streams. It sits on a branch above the water waiting for a fish to swim by. Then it dives beneath the surface and grabs or spears the fish with its beak. It also uses its beak to peck a hole for a nest in the river bank.

Otter

Otters are good swimmers. They are fast enough to catch fish and they will eat frogs and birds too. Otters make squeaking noises to each other.

When they are not hunting, otters like to play together on the river bank. Baby otters are called kits.

Catfish

There are lots of different freshwater catfish, big and small. They look as though they have cat's whiskers, but these are really feelers called barbels. As the fish swim along the riverbed they use their barbels to feel through the mud for food to eat.

Crocodile

Crocodiles live in warm parts of the world.
They float silently in rivers and water holes
looking for animals to catch and eat.
They have thick, scaly skin and sharp teeth.

Sometimes crocodiles crawl on to the
river bank to sunbathe or to lay eggs
in a nest they have dug.

Duck-billed platypus

This strange-looking creature lives in Australia. It has a beak like a duck, silky, soft fur and four big feet that look like paddles. When it dives under water it closes its eyes and ears and uses its beak to feel along the riverbed for food. It eats crabs, watersnails and worms.

Beaver

Beavers gnaw through trees with their sharp teeth. They use the branches to build a big wall across the river where they live. This is called a dam.

Behind the dam the water spreads out to become a big pool. The beavers build a nest of twigs to live in, called a lodge.

Heron

The tall heron stands as still as a statue
in ponds and pools, waiting for fish
or frogs to swim by. It stands so quietly
that the fish don't notice the danger
until it is too late. The heron thrusts
its sharp beak down quickly and snatches
the fish from the water.

Crab

Freshwater crabs are hard to spot because they hide among pond weed or under stones. On their front legs they have large claws which they use for eating.

When they come out to look for food they walk sideways. The female crabs lay lots of little eggs that hatch as tiny baby crabs.

Dragonfly

Dragonflies live near ponds and streams
looking for other insects to catch and eat.
They have very big eyes, two pairs
of thin wings and a fierce-looking mouth
for biting their food. Dragonflies can
hover in the air, turn around or dive
down quickly to chase something.

Water vole

Water voles live on river banks. They look like mice but they are much better swimmers. They are always busy, scurrying here and there looking for food.

They build themselves a cosy riverside nest lined with grass where they can hide away from hungry enemies such as owls.

Bullfrog

Bullfrogs can live in the water and on land. They have long, powerful back legs which they use to jump high in the air. They also have webbed feet for swimming. Bullfrogs have slimy skin so that they are nasty to eat. They have bulging eyes and make a loud croaking noise.

Where they live

This map of the world shows you where the animals live.

NORTH AMERICA

SOUTH AMERICA

 trout

kingfisher

otter

catfish

crocodile

platypus

beaver

heron

crab

dragonfly

water vole

bullfrog

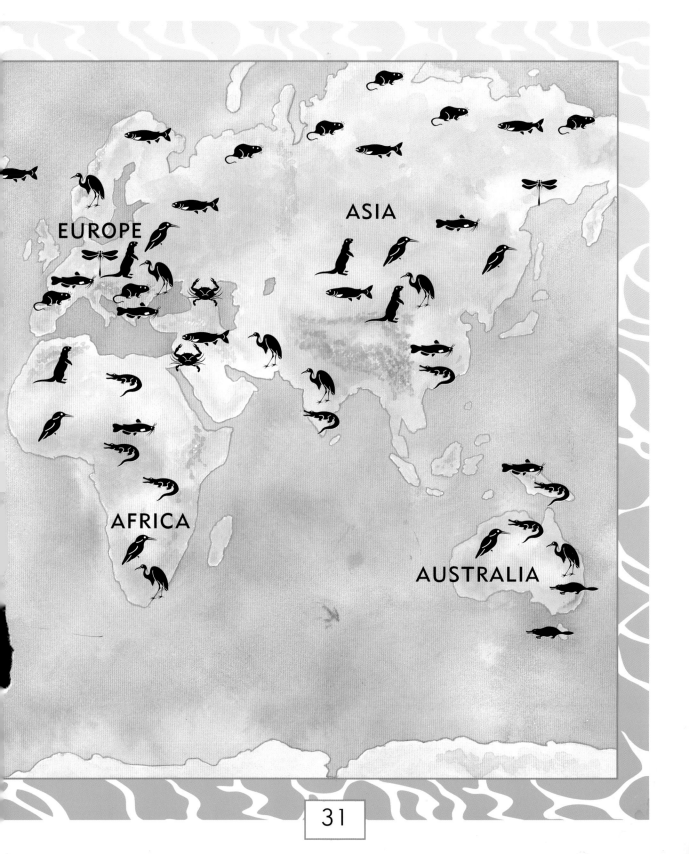

EUROPE

ASIA

AFRICA

AUSTRALIA

Index of words to learn

hatch to be born from an egg 7, 23

hover to hang in the air without moving
backwards or forwards 25

river bank the side of a river. It is often
made of mud 9, 11, 15

riverbed the bottom of a river. It can
be muddy or stony 7, 13, 17

stream a small river 9, 25

water hole a big pond 15

webbed feet feet with pieces of skin between
the toes. They help an animal to swim . . 29